To the Altar With God:
Prayers and Declarations for Engaged Couples

Tatiana Codner

Copyright © 2024 Tatiana Codner.

All rights reserved. No part of this book may be used or reproduced in any form whatsoever without written permission except in the case of brief quotations in critical articles or reviews.

Scripture quotations marked NLT are taken from the Holy Bible, New Living Translation, copyright © 1996, 2004, 2015 by Tyndale House Foundation. Used by permission of Tyndale House Publishers, Inc., Carol Stream, Illinois 60188. All rights reserved.

Scripture quotations marked NKJV are taken from the New King James Version®. Copyright © 1982 by Thomas Nelson. Used by permission. All rights reserved.

Scripture quotations marked TPT are from The Passion Translation®. Copyright © 2017, 2018, 2020 by Passion & Fire Ministries, Inc. Used by permission. All rights reserved. ThePassionTranslation.com.

Scripture quotations marked NIV are taken from the Holy Bible, New International Version®, NIV®. Copyright © 1973, 1978, 1984, 2011 by Biblica, Inc.™ Used by permission of Zondervan. All rights reserved worldwide. www.zondervan.com. The "NIV" and "New International Version" are trademarks registered in the United States Patent and Trademark Office by Biblica, Inc.™

Scripture quotations marked AMP are taken from the Amplified® Bible (AMP), Copyright © 2015 by The Lockman Foundation. Used by permission. lockman.org.

Scripture quotations marked AMPC are taken from the Amplified® Bible (AMPC), Copyright © 1954, 1958, 1962, 1964, 1965, 1987 by The Lockman Foundation. Used by permission. lockman.org.

Scripture quotations taken from the (NASB®) New American Standard Bible®, Copyright © 1960, 1971, 1977, 1995, 2020 by The Lockman Foundation. Used by permission. All rights reserved. lockman.org

Printed in the United States of America
Cover design by Leo Smith
ISBN - Paperback: 979-8-218-36080-1

Dedication

To Jesus Christ, my Lord and Savior, and to the Holy Spirit with whom I partnered to write this book. To my loving husband who has made me the most fulfilled wife, and to my parents who raised me to be the woman I am.

TABLE OF CONTENTS

INTRODUCTION 1

PART 1: PREPARING TO PRAY AND DECLARE 3
    Areas of Focus During Engagement Season 4
    The Importance of Praying as an Engaged Couple 8
    The Importance of Declaring as an Engaged Couple 11

PART 2: PRAYERS AND DECLARATIONS 15
    I. Gratitude for Relationship and Engagement 16
    II. Mercy 18
    III. Closeness With the Holy Spirit and Grace in a New Season 20
    IV. Character 22
    V. Forgiving Each Other 24
    VI. Unity and Agreement With Each Other 26
    VII. Learning About My Fiancé/Fiancée 28
    VIII. Healing from Emotional Trauma 30
    IX. Deliverance from Generational Curses and Releasing Generational Blessings 32
    X. Guidance and Wisdom 35
    XI. Peace and No Stress 38
    XII. Joy 40
    XIII. Grace for Wedding Planning and Order 42
    XIV. Financial Blessings, Favor, and Knowledge 45
    XV. Glorifying God on Our Wedding Day 48

XVI. Joining Our Families	50
XVII. Bridal Party	52
XVIII. Officiants and Counselors	55
XIX. Guests and Gift Givers	58
XX. Vendors	60
XXI. Beautiful Day/ Weather	63
XXII. Physical and Spiritual Territories	65
XXIII. A Beautiful and Glorious Marriage and Legacy	68

Introduction

Dear Engaged Couple,

Congratulations on your engagement! The Lord has been faithful to bring you to this season, and He will give you the grace to enjoy every moment of it. God is doing wonders through Kingdom marriages, and I am so excited for you to experience the gift that is partnering with your spouse to manifest the Kingdom of God on earth. I pray that you have had time to thoroughly embrace the excitement of your engagement season being here. For most people, the day they get engaged is a day they dream of, and yours has come! Now it is time to do the necessary work to make your engagement season fruitful, fulfilling, and enjoyable. This book will help you do just that.

Communicating with God during your engagement season is essential! While it is an exciting and joyous time, it is also a time of much transition and planning, and without the help of God, it can get overwhelming. I can attest that prayer helped me maintain focus and peace during my engagement, and I am writing this book to inspire other engaged couples to put prayer at the forefront of their road to the altar.

After our proposal, my then-fiancé and I sat down together and made a list of things we were praying for and praying against. We revisited this list throughout our engagement and trusted God to bring our prayers to pass — and indeed, He did! Our bridal party also interceded for us in the months leading up to our wedding day. We know that it is through prayer and intercession that we had a GLORIOUS wedding season.

This book contains an arsenal of powerful prayers and declarations to pray and declare individually and in agreement with your partner during your engagement. The prayer topics cover everything from spiritual growth and learning more about your partner to your bridal party and your wedding day. Along with each prayer topic are focus scriptures and declarations to which you can add your own, as declaring the Word of God is crucial to having the victory. I pray that these prayers and declarations will fortify you and encourage you as you continue on this beautiful journey!

Part I

Preparing to Pray and Declare

Areas of Focus During Engagement Season

The season of engagement begins after the proposal and is the turning point from dating or courting to becoming a married couple. During your engagement season, there should be four main areas of focus.

First, you should continue to deepen and sharpen your relationship with Jesus. When I got engaged, I received the advice that I should pray even more than I already do. It was great advice. 1 Peter 5:8 (KJV) instructs us: "Be sober, be vigilant; because your adversary the devil, as a roaring lion, walketh about, seeking whom he may devour." It is imperative that we don't forget our need for the voice of God even in the best of seasons because the moment we fail to seek God first, we inhibit our ability to hear His instructions clearly. You will surely need God's guidance as you go from engagement to marriage, so be sure to continue to pray and communicate with God daily. As led by the Holy Spirit, you should also set times of fasting to ask God for grace to succeed in engagement and in marriage.

Second, you should continue to develop and improve your character. To say you are ready to be married is to say you are ready to be selfless, mature, and forgiving each and every day. A good way to determine the areas in which your character needs improvement is to evaluate the relationships you have with other people in your life. Do you struggle to make sacrifices to help family members and friends? Do you find it difficult to forgive when people upset you? Do you speak up and communicate when you feel offended or do you remain quiet and hold grudges? Do you find it hard to take correction from or submit to authority? Are you loyal to your family members and friends or do you speak poorly about people behind their backs? Are you willing to be honest and transparent even when it is difficult? How does your character align with the definitions of love in 1 Corinthians 13:4-7? Asking and evaluating all of these questions is critical, and you should pray and ask God to highlight to you the areas in which your character needs improvement.

Third, you should get to know your partner more and more through transparent discussions and counseling sessions. No matter how much you were able to learn about your spouse during your dating season, there is always more to learn during your engagement season. Because engagement signals a serious commitment to getting married, it opens the door to deeper discussions with your partner. Engagement season is the time to learn it all, from what your partner fears in the relationship to what your expectations are when it comes to the division of labor. Engagement season is the time to practice transparency. You should not enter your marriage with anything hidden, but everything should be laid out and discussed. Other than a foundation in Christ, communication is the most important aspect of your marriage — even more important than love is. You can deeply love your partner, but if you are not willing to be emotionally open, honest, and transparent with your partner, the intimacy and understanding is lost and the marriage will fall apart. In addition to having one-on-one private discussions, it is imperative that you find a capable, Christian marriage counselor who can facilitate fruitful conversations on topics ranging from commitment to finances to sex.

All in all, engagement is a time during which God by His grace continues to impart to you the wisdom and understanding needed to succeed in your marriage. James 1:5 (NLT) says "If you need wisdom, ask our generous God, and he will give it to you. He will not rebuke you for asking." God is invested in your marriage succeeding because marriage is the system that God uses to orchestrate His will in the Earth. Even more, marriage is a representation of the covenant relationship between Christ and the church — His bride. When we understand the depth of the covenant relationship Jesus seeks to have with His church, we understand the depth of the covenant we are making in marriage.

Marriage is a serious commitment into which we should not enter without much prayer. It takes the grace of God for two people from two walks of life with two backgrounds and experiences to truly become one, and that is the essence of the beauty of marriage — two becoming one under Christ. Marriage can only succeed with God, for marriage was God's design and God's idea. In Genesis 2:18 (NLT), God Himself said, "It is not good for the man to be alone. I will make a helper who is just right for him." The Lord God in His wisdom and foresight saw from the beginning that a man could not succeed alone, but that he needed a woman to help him. God uses the marriages He ordains to fulfill His desire, which is that men and women will work together to spread the Gospel and raise Kingdom children who will do the same. Thus, we need His direction and guidance in all things concerning our marriage, including our engagement season.

Last but not least, the fourth area of focus is wedding planning! Wedding planning can be tricky to navigate without focus, sober-mindedness, and support. No matter how "big or small" your wedding will be, it will involve many moving parts, including the bridal party, the vendors, the venue, etc., and it is important for you to involve God in all of those details! Although the wedding lasts for a day or a weekend and marriage lasts for a lifetime, the wedding is not to be taken lightly. According to a couple's desires and the revelation they've had about the purpose for their marriage, the wedding day is a highly spiritual day on which the glory of God can be displayed. Furthermore, by the grace of God, your wedding planning and wedding day can be a blessing to many other people, like your parents, your bridal party, your vendors, and your guests. Your wedding is not all about you — it is also about all of the people who have supported you, surrounded you, and seen your love story flourish. It is important to intentionally commit your wedding planning to God in prayer.

The Importance of Praying as an Engaged Couple

Prayer is two-way communication between God and man. In 2 Timothy 1:12 (NLT), Apostle Paul made a powerful statement in his letter to Timothy. He said, "I am sure that [God] is able to guard what I have entrusted to him until the day of his return." The TPT version reads, "And my faith in him convinces me that he is more than able to keep all that I've placed in his hands safe and secure until the fullness of his appearing." As children of God, it is important to understand that for God to move powerfully and consistently in our lives, we have to give everything that we do into His hands. Just as only one person can drive a car at a time, only one person can be the driver of your life at a time. We cannot try to maintain control of everything and then seek God's blessings after decisions and moves have already been made. Paul caught the revelation that God is worth trusting because He is able to keep the things we commit to Him. Among the things we commit to God should certainly be the relationships He has blessed us with.

It is important to pray as an engaged couple to show God that you are committing every aspect of your engagement to Him. In Philippians 4:6-7, Apostle Paul admonishes us to be anxious for nothing, but in EVERYTHING by prayer and supplication with thanksgiving to let our requests be made known to God. Paul says that when we do that, the peace of

God, which surpasses all understanding, will guard our hearts and minds in Christ Jesus. When we pray, we give control to God, we invite Him to intervene in our situations, and we avail our ears to hear His instructions. When we pray, we evict anxiety and stress. In a season like engagement when you are not only preparing to make the significant commitment of marriage but also preparing to transition other aspects of your life, whether it be moving out of your parents' home or moving across the country, it is very important that you limit the reach of anxiety and stress. The Lord is willing and able to rid us of every worry, but we need to intentionally spend time in prayer. The Lord wants your engagement and wedding planning to succeed by His strength, but there is no such success without surrender.

It is also important to pray as an engaged couple to establish agreement in the realms of the spirit. In Matthew 18:19-20 (NLT), Jesus says, "I also tell you this: If two of you agree here on earth concerning anything you ask, my Father in heaven will do it for you. For where two or three gather together as my followers, I am there among them." Prayer is even more powerful when it is done in agreement with another person and when it is rooted in the Word of God. For each prayer topic in this book, there are accompanying scriptures that will help to establish the prayer in the Word of God. Whether you are continuing or just beginning your prayer journey with your partner, it is never ever too late to invite God to take control so that He will be glorified and so that your relationship can be a billboard for His glory. It is necessary and important to pray so that we remain focused on and yielded to the will of God. We are to "pray in the Spirit on all occasions with all kinds of prayers and requests," Ephesians 6:18 (NIV), so don't stop praying.

The Importance of Declaring as an Engaged Couple

A declaration is a statement or announcement that is backed by the power of the Scriptures. The Scriptures in the Bible are powerful. Hebrews 4:12 (NLT) reads, "For the word of God is alive and powerful. It is sharper than the sharpest two-edged sword, cutting between soul and spirit, between joint and marrow. It exposes our innermost thoughts and desires." Although the Bible was written centuries ago, it is very much still alive and active. This life that we live is full of spiritual battles. Satan, our enemy, is not pleased when we fulfill God's will for our lives or fulfill our Kingdom mandate which is to know Christ and to make Him known to others. Not only does Satan tempt us with sin to draw a wedge between us and God but he also pushes the spirit of fear on us so that our minds will not be at peace and so that we will be crippled and stagnant instead of stepping out on faith and fulfilling our Kingdom mandate. In Matthew 4:4, in response to being tempted by the devil, Jesus himself repeats the scripture written in Deuteronomy 8:3 (NKJV) – "man shall not live by bread alone; but man lives by every word that proceeds from the mouth of the LORD." Even Jesus utilized the power of the Word of God against Satan. In doing so, He shows us the weight and significance of God's Word.

Satan opposes anything that we do for God. In Ephesians 6:11-12 (NIV), Paul admonishes us: "Put on the full armor of God, so that you can take your stand against the devil's schemes. For our struggle is not against flesh and blood, but against the rulers, against the authorities, against the powers of this dark world and against the spiritual forces of evil in the heavenly realms." The resistance that you face or the battles that you fight in this life are not mere happenstance, but they are the manifestation of spiritual activity that took place beforehand. When Satan brews evil things in the spirit realm, we can use the Word of God to counteract and abort all of his plans. (Hosea 9:14)

One of Satan's greatest schemes is to lie to us. He plants lies in our minds and orchestrates circumstances that will cause us to believe that we will fail. He specializes in using lies and mind games. In fact, in John 8:44 (NLT), Jesus says of the devil, "He has always hated the truth, because there is no truth in him. When he lies, it is consistent with his character; for he is a liar and the father of lies." Everything that Satan says is said with deceptive intent. He figures that if he succeeded in deceiving Eve, then he can continually succeed in deceiving us. The word "deceive" literally means causing someone to believe something that is not true in order to gain some personal advantage over them. So that Satan does not take advantage of us, we must remain informed about his devices. 2 Corinthians 2:11.

This revelation knowledge is not to discourage us or make us afraid, for the Scriptures tell us that we already have the victory through Jesus. Romans 8:36-37 (NKJV) reads, "As it is written: 'For Your sake we are killed all day long; We are accounted as sheep for the slaughter.' Yet in all these things we are more than conquerors through Him who loved us." We already have the mandate to be conquerors, but we have to wrestle so that we will not be overcome by Satan's deceptions.

So how do we fight Satan and win? We fight using the spiritual weapons listed in Ephesians 6:14-17. Among the weapons is the sword of the Spirit, which is the Word of God. We win by decreeing and declaring the Word of God, marking our spiritual territory with declarations of victory that will stand forever just as lions mark their territory with their roar. Isaiah 40:8 (NLT) reads "The grass withers and the flowers fade, but the word of our God stands forever." When we declare the Word of God, it does not expire, but it stands for generations and generations. We see this with the covenants that God made with people in the Bible. For example, in 2 Samuel 7:12-13 (NKJV), God made the following covenant with David: "When your days are fulfilled and you rest with your fathers, I will set up your seed after you, who will come from your body, and I will establish his kingdom. He shall build a house for My name, and I will establish the throne of his kingdom forever." This promise is fulfilled generations and generations later in the coming and reign of Jesus Christ.

We can declare the Word of God over our present and over our future, and it will stand. The Bible says in Job 22:28 (NKJV) "You will also declare a thing, And it will be established for you; So light will shine on your ways." Declarations are a powerful tool to stamp the Word of God in our hearts and minds. Proverbs 18:21 (AMP) reads, "Death and life are in the power of the tongue, And those who love it and indulge it will eat its fruit and bear the consequences of their words." The more we declare the Word of God, the more we will experience the fullness of a God-filled life.

As an engaged couple, it is necessary and important to use declarations to mark your territory and to ensure that you will have victory in your now and in your future. Herein, there are declarations to accompany the prayer points and you can certainly add your own declarations backed by Scripture.

Part 2

Prayers and Declarations

I. Gratitude for Relationship and Engagement

Dear Father, Thank You for Your grace and mercy. From the beginning, You created relationships to bring glory to Your name, and we thank You for bringing us to this stage in our own relationship. Thank you for allowing us to meet and for Your grace that has kept us together. Thank You for bringing Your will for our relationship to pass at the right time. Thank You that as we go through our engagement season, You are molding and making us into the husband and wife that You desire us to be. Thank You for making this season possible. As we prepare to commit to each other for the rest of our lives, thank You Holy Spirit for guiding us and giving us courage and wisdom. We thank You for the gift of love and for this companionship. Thank You for allowing us to experience Your favor this far. Thank You for our season of establishment and celebration. We commit this season of our lives totally to You. We glorify You and build this altar of thanksgiving unto You. In the name of Jesus, Amen.

Scriptures
- I will bless the Lord at all times: his praise shall continually be in my mouth. Psalms 34:1 KJV
- Then Samuel took a stone and set it up between Mizpah and Shen, and called its name Ebenezer, saying, "Thus far the Lord has helped us." 1 Samuel 7:12 NKJV
- Then the Lord God said, "It is not good for the man to be alone. I will make a helper who is just right for him." Genesis 2:18 NLT
- Yet God has made everything beautiful for its own time. He has planted eternity in the human heart, but even so, people

cannot see the whole scope of God's work from beginning to end. Ecclesiastes 3:11 NLT

Declarations
- We decree and declare that we will bless the Lord at all times through our engagement and in our marriage.
- We decree and declare that challenges will not cause us to forfeit our thanksgiving.
- We decree and declare that we will be thankful in every season and circumstance.
- We decree and declare that we will bless the Lord at all times and speak of the great things He has done for us.

II. Mercy

Dear Father, help us to gain a deeper revelation of Your mercy in this season. It is only by Your mercy that we are alive and that we have entered into our season of marital breakthrough. We know that it is not by our own strength or might, but that it is by Your Spirit that we can overcome the forces that fight Kingdom marriages. You have shown us mercy and for that we are incredibly grateful. Lord, we know that we fall short of Your standard knowingly and unknowingly and that we will not be perfect in our efforts to please and honor You in all that we do. But we also know that if we confess our faults to You, You are faithful and just to forgive and cleanse us. We confess our transgressions, sins, and iniquities to You, and we ask for Your mercy. We pray that You release the Spirit of the fear of the Lord over us so that we and the generations that come from our union may dwell in Your righteousness and in holiness forever and ever. Thank You for showing us mercy. In the name of Jesus, Amen.

<u>Scriptures</u>
- So he answered and said to me: "This is the word of the Lord to Zerubbabel: 'Not by might nor by power, but by My Spirit,' Says the Lord of hosts." Zechariah 4:6 NKJV
- So then [God's gift] is not a question of human will and human effort, but of God's mercy. [It depends not on one's own willingness nor on his strenuous exertion as in running a race, but on God's having mercy on him]. Romans 9:16 AMPC
- For all have sinned, and come short of the glory of God. Romans 3:23 KJV

- If we say that we have no sin, we deceive ourselves, and the truth is not in us. If we confess our sins, He is faithful and just to forgive us our sins and to cleanse us from all unrighteousness. 1 John 1:8-9 NKJV
- Have mercy upon me, O God, According to Your lovingkindness; According to the multitude of Your tender mercies, Blot out my transgressions. Wash me thoroughly from my iniquity, And cleanse me from my sin. Psalms 51:1-2 NKJV
- Surely goodness and mercy shall follow me all the days of my life: and I will dwell in the house of the LORD for ever. Psalms 23:6 KJV
- Bless the Lord, O my soul: and all that is within me, bless his holy name. Bless the Lord, O my soul, and forget not all his benefits: Who forgiveth all thine iniquities; who healeth all thy diseases. Psalms 103:1-3 KJV

Declarations
- We decree and declare that we will walk in the Spirit of the fear of the Lord at all times.
- We decree and declare that we will never lose awareness of God's mercy and His many benefits toward us.
- We decree and declare that goodness and mercy will follow us all the days of our lives together.

III. Closeness With the Holy Spirit and Grace in a New Season

Dear Father, thank You for the gift of the precious Holy Spirit. We know that You have given us the Holy Spirit as our Helper, and we pray that You will give us the grace to grow closer to the Holy Spirit in this new season. We need the help of the Holy Spirit to stay focused and sober-minded. We pray for the grace to stay away from sin and to overcome any temptations that will inhibit our fellowship with the Holy Spirit. Give us the wisdom to walk in holiness so that we will not grieve the Holy Spirit. Lord, we ask that You will give us ears to hear the promptings of the Holy Spirit concerning our purpose together. Empower us to rebuke every false whisper of Satan, and help us to grow in the Holy Spirit, through which we obtain the fruit of love, joy, peace, forbearance, kindness, goodness, faithfulness, gentleness, and self-control. Lord, we ask that You make our hearts a home where the Holy Spirit can dwell. Help us to pray always in the Spirit for each other and for everything that concerns us. We ask that You use our relationship as a billboard for Your glory. Holy Spirit, remain with us in every step of this season, and allow us to feel Your tangible presence. Holy Spirit, we invite You to make Your home in our lives as we prepare to join as one. Come and take complete control of everything we seek to do. In the name of Jesus, Amen.

Scriptures
- And I will ask the Father, and He will give you another Helper (Comforter, Advocate, Intercessor—Counselor, Strengthener, Standby), to be with you forever. John 14:16 AMP
- Likewise the Spirit also helps in our weaknesses. For we do not know what we should pray for as we ought, but the Spirit

- Himself makes intercession for us with groanings which cannot be uttered. Romans 8:26 NKJV
- But the fruit of the Spirit is love, joy, peace, longsuffering, kindness, goodness, faithfulness, gentleness, self-control. Against such there is no law. Galatians 5:22-23 NKJV
- "But you will receive power when the Holy Spirit comes upon you. And you will be my witnesses, telling people about me everywhere—in Jerusalem, throughout Judea, in Samaria, and to the ends of the earth." Acts 1:8 NLT
- God's marvelous grace has manifested in person, bringing salvation for everyone. This same grace teaches us how to live each day as we turn our backs on ungodliness and indulgent lifestyles, and it equips us to live self-controlled, upright, godly lives in this present age. Titus 2:11-12 TPT

Declarations
- We decree and declare that we will be able to discern and stay away from things that hinder our closeness with the Holy Spirit.
- We decree and declare that we will continuously humble ourselves under God's mighty hand so that He can purge us of anything that grieves the Holy Spirit.
- We decree and declare that we will include the Holy Spirit in every aspect of our lives, and in doing so, our union will bear much fruit for the glory of God.

IV. Character

Dear Father, we ask for Your help in our attitude and character. In a culture where dishonor is taken lightly and disrespect is rampant, help us to honor each other without compromise. Holy Spirit, help us to demonstrate a Christ-like attitude toward each other in every situation. Help us to be patient and to make an effort to understand each other in moments of disagreement. Help us to bridle our tongues in moments of frustration and demonstrate compassion and consideration in times of difficulty. Help us to humbly listen to each other's concerns and constructive criticisms without being disrespectful or defensive. We pray that we will always demonstrate honesty and openness even when we are nervous about how what we say will be received. Give us the grace to be set apart even in our very thoughts. Help us Lord to think true, honorable, pure, just, lovely, excellent, and praise-worthy thoughts about each other at all times. We cancel every spirit of pride, unforgiveness, competition, and disloyalty, and we declare that we will walk in Godly love. In the name of Jesus, Amen.

Scriptures
- Do not conform to the pattern of this world, but be transformed by the renewing of your mind. Then you will be able to test and approve what God's will is—his good, pleasing and perfect will. Romans 12:2 NIV
- And now, dear brothers and sisters, one final thing. Fix your thoughts on what is true, and honorable, and right, and pure, and lovely, and admirable. Think about things that are excellent and worthy of praise. Philippians 4:8 NLT
- May the God who gives endurance and encouragement give you the same attitude of mind toward each other that Christ

Jesus had, so that with one mind and one voice you may glorify the God and Father of our Lord Jesus Christ. Romans 15:5-6 NIV
- Love must be sincere. Hate what is evil; cling to what is good. Be devoted to one another in love. Honor one another above yourselves. Romans 12:9-10 NIV
- Do to others as you would like them to do to you. Luke 6:31 NLT

<u>Declarations</u>
- We decree and declare that we will not allow poor or ungodly character to divide us.
- We decree and declare that before we speak or act, we will consider the consequences of our words and actions.
- We decree and declare that we will submit to the process of our character being improved during our engagement season.

V. Forgiving Each Other

  Dear Father, we ask that You will impart to us the grace to forgive one another fully and quickly. We realize that forgiving one another is a command from You and not a choice. We also realize that if we do not forgive each other, our relationship with each other and our relationship with You will be hindered. Help us to treat each other with respect and honor and to put away bitterness, rage, anger, harsh words, slander, and every other kind of evil behavior that we may be practicing. Help us to be compassionate, kind, humble, gentle, and patient with one another, showing each other the same mercy and forgiveness that You show us daily. Holy Spirit, convict us when we are wrong, and give us the spirit of urgency to make things right. In this season of our engagement, as we learn more about each other and prepare for our wedding and marriage, help us to do away with offense and to clothe ourselves with forgiveness and mercy. In the name of Jesus, Amen.

<u>Scriptures</u>
- Blessed are the merciful: for they shall obtain mercy. Matthew 5:7 KJV
- "For if you forgive men their trespasses, your heavenly Father will also forgive you. But if you do not forgive men their trespasses, neither will your Father forgive your trespasses." Matthew 6:14-15 NKJV
- Get rid of all bitterness, rage, anger, harsh words, and slander, as well as all types of evil behavior. Instead, be kind to each other, tenderhearted, forgiving one another, just as God through Christ has forgiven you. Ephesians 4:31-32 NLT

- Therefore, as God's chosen people, holy and dearly loved, clothe yourselves with compassion, kindness, humility, gentleness and patience. Bear with each other and forgive one another if any of you has a grievance against someone. Forgive as the Lord forgave you. Colossians 3:12-13 NIV
- So if you are presenting a sacrifice at the altar in the Temple and you suddenly remember that someone has something against you, leave your sacrifice there at the altar. Go and be reconciled to that person. Then come and offer your sacrifice to God. Matthew 5:23-24 NLT

Declarations
- We decree and declare that we will grow in forgiveness all the days of our engagement and marriage.
- We decree and declare that compassion, kindness, humility, gentleness, and patience will reside in our relationship.
- We decree and declare that malice and strife will have no place in our hearts and in our home.

VI. Unity and Agreement With Each Other

Dear Father, we pray for the spirit of unity and agreement to fall on us. In a culture where independence is more valued than interdependence, help us to understand that You created us to complement, lean on, and walk with each other. Lord, You are the perfect example of unity, for God the Father, God the Son, and God the Holy Spirit dwell together in perfect fellowship and unity. As we prepare for marriage, help us to exercise unity starting now. Help us to understand that exercising unity and agreement does not mean that we are not allowed to have our own opinions, but that exercising unity and agreement means that we should submit our opinions to God in the proper order. (1 Corinthians 11:3) Lord, You taught us that a house divided against itself will not stand. Therefore, help us to be unified in our principles, values, and decision-making. Jesus, we decree and declare that we will be a couple that fulfills the prayer You prayed for us that we would be one with each other just as You are one with the Father. Thank You Lord Jesus for making it possible, through Your death and resurrection, for us to be reconciled with You. We pray that through our unity, we will show forth Your glory and draw others to You. In the name of Jesus, Amen.

Scriptures
- But Jesus knew their thoughts, and said to them: "Every kingdom divided against itself is brought to desolation, and every city or house divided against itself will not stand." Matthew 12:25 NKJV
- Be completely humble and gentle; be patient, bearing with one another in love. Make every effort to keep the unity of the Spirit through the bond of peace. Ephesians 4:2-3 NIV

- And the LORD God said, It is not good that the man should be alone; I will make him an help meet for him. Genesis 2:18 KJV
- A person standing alone can be attacked and defeated, but two can stand back-to-back and conquer. Three are even better, for a triple-braided cord is not easily broken. Ecclesiastes 4:12 NLT
- Can two people walk together without agreeing on the direction? Amos 3:3 NLT
- "My prayer is not for them alone. I pray also for those who will believe in me through their message, that all of them may be one, Father, just as you are in me and I am in you. May they also be in us so that the world may believe that you have sent me." John 17:20-21 NIV

Declarations
- We decree and declare that we will face life and its challenges as a united front and not as lone soldiers.
- We decree and declare that we will build trust with each other so that we become more comfortable sharing everything with each other.
- We decree and declare that division will not cause our downfall in Jesus' name.

VII. Learning About My Fiancé/Fiancée

Dear Father, thank You for blessing us with a loving and caring partner in each other. As we prepare to enter into our marriage, we pray that You will help us to learn everything we should learn about each other during our engagement. We realize that we are coming from two different backgrounds with two different experiences, which will inform how we understand and relate to one another. Help us to see each other not only through the lens of how we communicate now but also through the lens of the things we may have dealt with in our past. To that end, we pray for the spirit of honesty and transparency to be our portion at all times. Help us to open up to each other without fear of judgment. We pray that we will dwell with each other not just according to knowledge but also according to understanding and empathy. In addition to learning about our hobbies, interests, and favorite things, let us be ready to learn about the hardship, worries, and fears that we are working to let go of. Let self-centeredness be far away from us and authentic love be near us at all times. May we always endure difficult situations together, may we always listen and seek to understand before speaking, and may we not exalt the need to be right, but exalt the need to be unified. In the name of Jesus, Amen.

<u>Scriptures</u>
- Wisdom is the principal thing; Therefore get wisdom. And in all your getting, get understanding. Proverbs 4:7 NKJV
- Let each of you look out not only for his own interests, but also for the interests of others. Philippians 2:4 NKJV
- Fools have no interest in understanding; they only want to air their own opinions. Proverbs 18:2 NLT

- In the same way, you husbands must give honor to your wives. Treat your wife with understanding as you live together. She may be weaker than you are, but she is your equal partner in God's gift of new life. Treat her as you should so your prayers will not be hindered. 1 Peter 3:7 NLT
- Buy truth, and do not sell it; Get wisdom and instruction and understanding. Proverbs 23:23 AMP
- Love is patient and kind. Love is not jealous or boastful or proud or rude. It does not demand its own way. It is not irritable, and it keeps no record of being wronged. It does not rejoice about injustice but rejoices whenever the truth wins out. Love never gives up, never loses faith, is always hopeful, and endures through every circumstance. 1 Corinthians 13:4-7 NLT

Declarations
- We decree and declare that we will seek to understand each other and not judge each other.
- We decree and declare that we will rely on the help of the Holy Spirit to bear each other's burdens.
- We decree and declare that we will let the love of Christ guide our words and actions.

VIII. Healing from Emotional Trauma

Dear Father, all of our help comes from You. We pray that as we prepare to join as one, You heal us from the pain of any traumatic experiences we have been through. Lord, heal us from emotional scars known and unknown. Whether we've gone through childhood abuse, the loss of a loved one, a terrifying physical illness, failed relationships, or feelings of failure and rejection, we lay them all before You and ask that You heal us from the deep wounds we may be carrying. You know everything about us, and we trust that You will make our healing complete. God of all comfort, we pray that You will help us not to boast in any ability to mask pain, but to be vulnerable before You and to be honest with each other. We know that if we fail to acknowledge and heal from our pain, we will project it onto one another. Therefore Lord, we ask for Your healing power and deliverance from every brokenness that may threaten the peace in our union. Mend the areas of our spirit that may be crushed. Help us to trust each other fully and sincerely. Thank you Lord that we can cast all our burdens on You, and thank You for Your promise that we will not be moved. Thank You for bandaging our wounds and giving us cheerful hearts. In the name of Jesus, Amen.

<u>Scriptures</u>
- All praise to God, the Father of our Lord Jesus Christ. God is our merciful Father and the source of all comfort. He comforts us in all our troubles so that we can comfort others. When they are troubled, we will be able to give them the same comfort God has given us. 2 Corinthians 1:3-4 NLT

- O Lord, You have searched me and known me. You know my sitting down and my rising up; You understand my thought afar off. You comprehend my path and my lying down, And are acquainted with all my ways. For there is not a word on my tongue, But behold, O Lord, You know it altogether. Psalms 139:1-4 NKJV
- Cast your burden on the Lord, And He shall sustain you; He shall never permit the righteous to be moved. Psalms 55:22 NKJV
- He heals the brokenhearted and bandages their wounds. Psalms 147:3 NLT
- A cheerful heart is good medicine, but a broken spirit saps a person's strength. Proverbs 17:22 NLT

Declarations
- We decree and declare that our healing from emotional trauma breaks forth speedily in Jesus' name!
- We decree and declare that any emotional hurt will not hinder our union.
- We decree and declare that our hearts and minds are completely healed and whole. Thank You Jesus!

IX. Deliverance from Generational Curses and Releasing Generational Blessings

Dear Father, we thank You that You are a faithful and just God. Through Your Word, You have revealed that curses and blessings can be passed from generation to generation. But by Your mercy and through the death and resurrection of Jesus Christ, You have given us the ability to be rescued from every curse. Thank You Lord for the promise of a new identity in You. We only know a portion of our background, but You know the full background that we are coming from. Deliver us from the stain of any generational curses in our bloodlines. Disconnect us from any demonic altars or covenants that were raised by any of our ancestors. Help us to detach ourselves from any ungodly or unfruitful habits or traditions that have been passed down in our families. Lord, may we begin to unlearn any behaviors that could cause disunity or dysfunction in our marriage. Give us the grace to follow the pathway of righteousness rather than any unrighteous pathways that our forefathers have walked. Help us to intentionally write Your Word on the tablets of our hearts and to teach it to our children so that they will accept and serve Christ. Lord, we pray that generational blessings for a thousand generations will continue and begin with us. Thank You for hearing and answering our prayers. In the name of Jesus, Amen.

Scriptures
- You must not bow down to them or worship them, for I, the Lord your God, am a jealous God who will not tolerate your affection for any other gods. I lay the sins of the parents upon their children; the entire family is affected—even children in the third and fourth generations of those who reject me. But I lavish unfailing love for a thousand

generations on those who love me and obey my commands. Exodus 20:5-6 NLT
- Behold, every one that useth proverbs shall use this proverb against thee, saying, As is the mother, so is her daughter. Ezekiel 16:44 KJV
- Amon was twenty-two years old when he became king, and he reigned in Jerusalem two years. His mother was Meshullemeth, the daughter of Haruz from Jotbah. He did what was evil in the Lord's sight, just as his father, Manasseh, had done. He followed the example of his father, worshiping the same idols his father had worshiped. He abandoned the Lord, the God of his ancestors, and he refused to follow the Lord's ways. 2 Kings 21:19-22 NLT
- But Christ has rescued us from the curse pronounced by the law. When he was hung on the cross, he took upon himself the curse for our wrongdoing. For it is written in the Scriptures, "Cursed is everyone who is hung on a tree." Galatians 3:13 NLT
- So you have not received a spirit that makes you fearful slaves. Instead, you received God's Spirit when he adopted you as his own children. Now we call him, "Abba, Father." Romans 8:15 NLT
- For he issued his laws to Jacob; he gave his instructions to Israel. He commanded our ancestors to teach them to their children, so the next generation might know them—even the children not yet born—and they in turn will teach their own children. So each generation should set its hope anew on God, not forgetting his glorious miracles and obeying his commands. Then they will not be like their ancestors—stubborn, rebellious, and unfaithful, refusing to give their hearts to God. Psalms 78:5-8 NLT

Declarations
- We decree and declare that every generational curse ends with us, and any curse in our bloodline will not pass to the next generation in Jesus' name.
- We decree and declare that our union begins a new chapter of generational blessings in our bloodline.
- We decree and declare that generational curses are far from our children and generational blessings pursue them in Jesus' name!

X. Guidance and Wisdom

Dear Father, thank You for being a good Father. We need Your guidance as we journey through this new season in our lives. As a good earthly father guides his children down the right path, we know that You are guiding us and leading us in the way we should go. Lord, we pray that You will give us ears that hear Your instructions and hearts that willingly obey. As we make decisions, help us to trust in You with all our hearts instead of relying on our own understanding. Whenever we are at a crossroads, we pray that we will turn our ears to You for directions instead of turning to our own understanding or our past experiences. Lord, we stand on Your promises that You will lead us down a new path and guide us along an unfamiliar way. We thank You now that according to Your Word, You have lightened every dark place before us and You have smoothed every crooked road ahead of us. Lord, we know that the road before us will not always be easy, but You know the way that we take. Even in times of testing, we know that You are with us and holding our hands.

Father, we pray for an outpour of Godly wisdom in our lives. We ask that You help us make wise choices in every aspect of this engagement season. We pray for Your wisdom to guide us through every decision and every circumstance. We thank You now for an outpouring of Your wisdom, as You promise in Your Word that You give wisdom liberally and without reproach. Father, as we make decisions, give us discernment, for Your Word says that any wisdom coming from above is pure, peaceful, gentle, humble, merciful, full of good deeds, impartial and sincere. Lord, may we remember to assess every decision through this lens, understanding that You would not lead us astray. As we intentionally seek Your wisdom in this season, we pray that we will be blessed and joyful each and every day. We thank You for guiding us and pouring out Your wisdom. In the name of Jesus, Amen.

Scriptures
- Trust in the Lord with all your heart, And lean not on your own understanding; In all your ways acknowledge Him, And He shall direct your paths. Proverbs 3:5-6 NKJV
- Your ears shall hear a word behind you, saying, "This is the way, walk in it," Whenever you turn to the right hand or whenever you turn to the left. Isaiah 30:21 NKJV
- I will lead blind Israel down a new path, guiding them along an unfamiliar way. I will brighten the darkness before them and smooth out the road ahead of them. Yes, I will indeed do these things; I will not forsake them. Isaiah 42:16 NLT
- But He knows the way that I take; When He has tested me, I shall come forth as gold. Job 23:10 NKJV
- Blessed is a person who finds wisdom, And one who obtains understanding. Proverbs 3:13 NASB
- For the LORD gives wisdom; from his mouth come knowledge and understanding. Proverbs 2:6 NIV
- If any of you lacks wisdom [to guide him through a decision or circumstance], he is to ask of [our benevolent] God, who gives to everyone generously and without rebuke or blame, and it will be given to him. James 1:5 AMP
- But the wisdom from above is first of all pure. It is also peace loving, gentle at all times, and willing to yield to others. It is full of mercy and the fruit of good deeds. It shows no favoritism and is always sincere. James 3:17 NLT

Declarations
- We decree and declare that we will always seek to go God's way and not our own.

- We decree and declare that wisdom is our companion.
- We decree and declare that we will not despise God's instruction and rebuke, but welcome and appreciate it, knowing it keeps us on the right path.

XI. Peace and No Stress

Dear Father, we glorify and magnify You. We understand that when we magnify You, we make You bigger than anything we are facing, and we thank You that You are always with us. Lord, today we declare that we will not be shaken because You are always right beside us. In this season, we realize that there will be many situations that come to bring us stress. But today, we declare that peace will be our everlasting portion in this season and beyond. Lord, we realize that peace is not the absence of hostility, but peace is truly Your presence with us. You are the only One who can give us perfect peace when we keep our minds on You and trust in You. You are the only One who can give us peace that surpasses all understanding. Holy Spirit, we ask that as we go through preparation and planning, You will constantly remind us that we must reject anxiety and instead, by prayer and supplication, with thanksgiving, ask You for what we need.

Lord, we thank You for the assurance that in the midst of circumstances that tempt us to be anxious, we can pray and rest in Your promise of peace. We pray for an outpouring of Your precious Holy Spirit to flood our minds, for Your Word says that a mind governed by the Spirit is life and peace. Help us not to focus on our carnal understanding of things, but to seek Your face to know what You are saying about a matter. We know that marriage and wedding planning can come with a lot of pressure to please and impress others, but help us to remember that in all things, our focus should be to please and glorify You. As we navigate this season, we pray that You will help us to be peacemakers at all times. May we constantly be at peace with each other and with everyone around us. Lord, we rebuke every feeling of stress, anxiety, and worry, knowing that these emotions profit us nothing. Father, we give You all of our worries, and we stand and rely on Your Word. In the name of Jesus, Amen.

Scriptures
- I know the Lord is always with me. I will not be shaken, for he is right beside me. Psalms 16:8 NLT
- You will keep him in perfect peace, Whose mind is stayed on You, Because he trusts in You. Isaiah 26:3 NKJV
- Be anxious for nothing, but in everything by prayer and supplication, with thanksgiving, let your requests be made known to God; and the peace of God, which surpasses all understanding, will guard your hearts and minds through Christ Jesus. Philippians 4:6-7 NKJV
- The mind governed by the flesh is death, but the mind governed by the Spirit is life and peace. Romans 8:6 NIV
- Make every effort to live in peace with everyone and to be holy; without holiness no one will see the Lord. Hebrews 12:14 NIV
- Peacemakers who sow in peace reap a harvest of righteousness. James 3:18 NV
- Which of you by worrying can add one cubit to his stature? Matthew 6:27 NKJV
- Give all your worries and cares to God, for he cares about you. 1 Peter 5:7 NLT

Declarations
- We decree and declare that stress is not our portion!
- We decree and declare that anxiety is far from us.
- We decree and declare that peace reigns in our relationship, and the enemy will not sow seeds of discord and division here.

XII. Joy

Dear Father, we thank You for bringing us to this season of rejoicing and for turning our season of waiting into joyous celebration that our marital breakthrough is here. We know that it is only by Your mercy that we are walking into the promises that You have ordained for us. We have sown in prayers and now we are reaping with shouts of joy. Lord, we are grateful! We pray that You will give us the discipline to remain in Your presence throughout this engagement season so that we will experience the fullness of Your joy. We desire to experience Your joy – a joy that is everlasting, a joy that gives us strength, and a joy that glorifies You! We know that as long as we are joyful, we will be strong and able to stand against the attacks of the enemy.

Lord, we pray that our genuine joy will draw others to You. As our mouths are filled with laughter, may others join in our celebration and glorify You for the great things You have done for us. Lord, we pray that the spirit of the fear of the Lord will fall upon us so that we will obey Your commandments and abide in Your love and joy. We pray that no matter what challenges come our way, we will maintain our joy in You. We bind the spirits of sadness, heaviness, anxiety, weariness, and stress. Thank You Lord for overflowing and everlasting joy. In the name of Jesus, Amen.

Scriptures
- And Nehemiah continued, "Go and celebrate with a feast of rich foods and sweet drinks, and share gifts of food with people who have nothing prepared. This is a sacred day before our Lord. Don't be dejected and sad, for the joy of the LORD is your strength!" Nehemiah 8:10 NLT

- Be cheerful with joyous celebration in every season of life. Let your joy overflow! Philippians 4:4 TPT
- Those who plant in tears will harvest with shouts of joy. Psalms 126:5 NLT
- You will show me the path of life; In Your presence is fullness of joy; At Your right hand are pleasures forevermore. Psalms 16:11 NKJV
- "If you keep My commandments, you will abide in My love, just as I have kept My Father's commandments and abide in His love. These things I have spoken to you, that My joy may remain in you, and that your joy may be full." John 15:10-11 NKJV
- When the Lord restored the fortunes of Zion, we were like those who dreamed. Our mouths were filled with laughter, our tongues with songs of joy. Then it was said among the nations, "The Lord has done great things for them." The Lord has done great things for us, and we are filled with joy. Psalms 126:1-3 NIV

Declarations
- We decree and declare that the joy of the Lord is indeed our strength. Therefore we will never be weakened in Jesus' name!
- We decree and declare that we will magnify the reasons we have to rejoice.
- We decree and declare that we will remain at the right hand of God where our pleasures and provisions are.

XIII. Grace for Wedding Planning and Order

Dear Father, thank You for bringing us this far! We are grateful that we are at the stage in our journey where we can plan one of the days we have long-anticipated – the day we say our vows before You and officially become a married couple. We thank You that You already know the plans that You have for us on our wedding day. We commit our plans and desires to You, and we ask that Your purpose alone will stand. Lord, before we put pen to paper, we ask for Your grace and help as we plan. Holy Spirit, we ask that You would lead, guide, and direct us through all of the details and logistics. We pray that we will be led by You in all that we do and that we will not be led by the spirit of pride, offense, or self-righteousness.

Lord, help us to do what pleases You from the beginning to the end of our wedding day. We pray that all things will be done with care and intentionality rather than with haste. Father, we pray that everything on our wedding day will be carried out decently and in order. We bind any confusion that the enemy has released to frustrate or interrupt our wedding day or any of the days leading up to our wedding, and we release the spirit of order. We pray that we will be resourceful and submit to You in everything that we are doing, whether it be creating our guest list or picking various vendors. Let us seek to make choices that honor and please You rather than appeasing our flesh. Lord, we ask that You give us the strength to carry out every task amidst our existing commitments and responsibilities. Where we lack certain skills, we ask that You will grace us with those skills and lead us to get help from those who possess them. As we plan, help us to understand that while all things may not work out the way we anticipated, they are working out in a way that will work for our good. Lord, we pray that we will learn more about each other and grow closer as we discuss and make our plans. We thank You in advance for bringing our wedding day to perfect completion. In the name of Jesus, Amen.

Scriptures
- "For I know the plans I have for you," says the LORD. "They are plans for good and not for disaster, to give you a future and a hope." Jeremiah 29:11 NLT
- Many plans are in a man's mind, But it is the LORD's purpose for him that will stand (be carried out). Proverbs 19:21 AMP
- Commit your works to the LORD [submit and trust them to Him], And your plans will succeed [if you respond to His will and guidance]. Proverbs 16:3 AMP
- We can make our plans, but the LORD determines our steps. Proverbs 16:9 NLT
- Look here, you who say, "Today or tomorrow we are going to a certain town and will stay there a year. We will do business there and make a profit." How do you know what your life will be like tomorrow? Your life is like the morning fog—it's here a little while, then it's gone. What you ought to say is, "If the Lord wants us to, we will live and do this or that." Otherwise you are boasting about your own pretentious plans, and all such boasting is evil. James 4:13-16 NLT
- I can do all things through Christ who strengthens me. Philippians 4:13 NKJV
- Enthusiasm without knowledge is no good; haste makes mistakes. Proverbs 19:2 NLT
- For God is not a God of disorder but of peace—as in all the congregations of the Lord's people. 1 Corinthians 14:33 NIV

- But all things must be done appropriately and in an orderly manner. 1 Corinthians 14:40 AMP
- And we know that God causes everything to work together for the good of those who love God and are called according to his purpose for them. Romans 8:28 NLT

<u>Declarations</u>
- We decree and declare that we will not succumb to the stresses of wedding planning, but we will keep our minds focused on the big picture, which is glorifying God.
- We decree and declare that we are graced by God for the season that we are in.
- We decree and declare that the Holy Spirit is in complete control of our wedding day in Jesus' name.

XIV. Financial Blessings, Favor, and Knowledge

Dear Father, we thank You that You have blessed us with every spiritual blessing. Because You are a good Father and our Shepherd, we are already blessed beyond measure. Lord, as we go through this engagement and wedding planning season, we pray that You will allow us to experience favor and financial blessings in abundance. Help us to exercise wisdom and to budget and plan according to our means, while also believing and understanding that You are able to do exceedingly, abundantly, and above all we could ever ask or think. Help us to maintain a heart that gives cheerfully and freely at all times, for You admonish us to be cheerful givers. During this season, we pray that we will experience supernatural favor wherever we go and that You will bless us so that we have more than enough to bless others. We thank You that we do not need to worry about anything because You know what we need before we even ask for it. As we delight ourselves in You, we pray that You will grant us our heart's desires.

Lord, we also ask that You give us a desire to acquire financial knowledge. As we prepare to be married and start a family, help us to begin to learn the ways in which we can leave our children an inheritance. We pray that we will always be ready to learn and that our ears will always be open for knowledge. We pray for the discipline to spend and save effectively, and we pray that we will remember to seek out resources that will teach us about the ways to build generational wealth, such as investing in the stock market or in real estate. We pray that You will reveal our skills and talents to us and give us the insight and discipline to monetize them. Lord, fill us with the Spirit of God that brings great wisdom, ability, and expertise in various crafts and give us

Kingdom business ideas that will glorify You. We come against the spirits of laziness, self-doubt, procrastination, and delay that will try to hinder us from building financial wealth. We pray that we will be submitted to the leading of Your Spirit in all things and that Your beauty will come upon us and establish the work of our hands. In the name of Jesus, Amen.

Scriptures
- All praise to God, the Father of our Lord Jesus Christ, who has blessed us with every spiritual blessing in the heavenly realms because we are united with Christ. Ephesians 1:3 NLT
- The LORD is my shepherd; I have all that I need. Psalms 23:1 NLT
- Now all glory to God, who is able, through his mighty power at work within us, to accomplish infinitely more than we might ask or think. Ephesians 3:20 NLT
- Surely, LORD, you bless the righteous; you surround them with your favor as with a shield. Psalms 5:12 NIV
- You must each decide in your heart how much to give. And don't give reluctantly or in response to pressure. "For God loves a person who gives cheerfully." And God will generously provide all you need. Then you will always have everything you need and plenty left over to share with others. 2 Corinthians 9:7-8 NLT
- Intelligent people are always ready to learn. Their ears are open for knowledge. Proverbs 18:15 NLT
- Good people leave an inheritance to their grandchildren, but the sinner's wealth passes to the godly. Proverbs 13:22 NLT
- Then Moses told the people of Israel, "The Lord has specifically chosen Bezalel son of Uri, grandson of Hur, of the tribe of Judah. The Lord has filled Bezalel with the Spirit

of God, giving him great wisdom, ability, and expertise in all kinds of crafts." Exodus 35:30-31 NLT
- Good planning and hard work lead to prosperity, but hasty shortcuts lead to poverty. Proverbs 21:5 NLT
- Professional work habits prevent poverty from becoming your permanent business partner. And: If you put off until tomorrow the work you could do today, tomorrow never seems to come. Proverbs 24:33-34 TPT
- And let the beauty of the Lord our God be upon us, And establish the work of our hands for us; Yes, establish the work of our hands. Psalms 90:17 NKJV

Declarations
- We declare that the Lord is the source of all our provision and wealth.
- We decree and declare that we will walk in our God-given capacity to create wealth.
- We decree and declare that lack is far from us in Jesus' name!
- We decree and declare that we are not intimidated by financial knowledge, but our minds are equipped to learn and understand it.

XV. Glorifying God on Our Wedding Day

Dear Father, we thank You for Your grace, mercy, and favor on our lives. We thank You that You have not only ordained our marriage, but You have also ordained our wedding day to bring glory and honor to You. As we prepare to stand before You, our family, and our friends to be joined as one, we pray that Your presence will go ahead of us. We pray that You will make every crooked place straight and break every resistance or contention in the name of Jesus. Lord, only You deserve the glory and honor for what is happening in our lives. In Your great mercy and sovereignty, You put us together, and we want our wedding to glorify You alone. We commit our wedding ceremony to You, and we pray that everything we do will point people to You. This is all for Your glory, and we give You thanks.

Lord, as we carry Your Spirit with us, we pray that anyone who encounters us on our wedding day and thereafter will feel Your reassuring love. May those who do not have a personal relationship with You be drawn to You. Lord, as You make Your face shine upon us, help us to represent You well in all that we do on our wedding day. We pray that everyone who encounters us on our wedding day will encounter Your light that drives out darkness. Help us to radiate Your glory Lord, and give us the discipline to arise and shine as we walk together. In the name of Jesus, Amen.

<u>Scriptures</u>
- I will go before you And make the crooked places straight; I will break in pieces the gates of bronze And cut the bars of iron. Isaiah 45:2 NKJV

- Not to us, O LORD, not to us, but to your name goes all the glory for your unfailing love and faithfulness. Psalms 115:1 NLT
- So whether you eat or drink, or whatever you do, do it all for the glory of God. 1 Corinthians 10:31 NLT
- Whatever you do [no matter what it is] in word or deed, do everything in the name of the Lord Jesus [and in dependence on Him], giving thanks to God the Father through Him. Colossians 3:17 AMP
- Do you not know that you are the temple of God and that the Spirit of God dwells in you? 1 Corinthians 3:16 NKJV
- Let your light shine before men in such a way that they may see your good deeds and moral excellence, and [recognize and honor and] glorify your Father who is in heaven. Matthew 5:16 AMP
- The LORD bless thee, and keep thee: The LORD make his face shine upon thee, and be gracious unto thee: The LORD lift up his countenance upon thee, and give thee peace. Numbers 6:24-26 KJV
- So God created man in his own image, in the image of God created he him; male and female created he them. Genesis 1:27 KJV
- Arise, shine; for thy light is come, and the glory of the LORD is risen upon thee. Isaiah 60:1 KJV

Declarations
- We decree and declare that Jesus Christ will be glorified on our wedding day and in our marriage.
- We decree and declare that any spirit that exalts itself above Christ will be brought low in Jesus' name.
- We decree and declare that the light of Christ shining through us will bring people to salvation in Jesus' name.

XVI. Joining Our Families

Dear Lord, we thank You for the families You placed us in that have raised us to be where we are now. We are grateful that by Your grace, You have picked us out from two families to create a family of our own. This is Your marvelous doing, and we are grateful! We pray that as You join us together in marriage, You also join our families together as one. We desire the spirit of unity and compassion to be our family's portion. Help us to now love and relate to our in-laws as family members of our very own. We rebuke any winds of contention and confusion that may divide our family, and we pray that our family members will be of one mind.

Above all, Lord, we pray that the spirit of love will bind our families together. May our family members always exercise compassion and courtesy toward one another. When we gather as one big family, may there be no bitterness, rage, anger, harsh words, slander, or any other type of evil behavior. We come against arguments and unhealthy debates, and we pray that we will always have a reason to celebrate. We pray that our marriage will be a great blessing to our family members, and that it will birth divine connections and destiny relationships in our families.

We pray that as we come together as one and as we leave our separate homes, You will give us the grace to establish healthy boundaries. May we honor our families in a healthy way, while never allowing their words or opinions to sow any unhealthy seeds in our union. May we never paint each other in a poor light in the midst of our family, but may we always be a unified front. Lord, we thank You now for joining our families together in peace. We give You glory and praise. In Jesus' name, Amen.

Scriptures
- How wonderful and pleasant it is when brothers live together in harmony! Psalms 133:1 NLT
- This is the LORD's doing; It is marvellous in our eyes. Psalms 118:23 KJV
- Finally, all [of you] should be of one and the same mind (united in spirit), sympathizing [with one another], loving [each other] as brethren [of one household], compassionate and courteous (tenderhearted and humble). 1 Peter 3:8 AMPC
- Above all, clothe yourselves with love, which binds us all together in perfect harmony. Colossians 3:14 NLT
- Get rid of all bitterness, rage, anger, harsh words, and slander, as well as all types of evil behavior. Instead, be kind to each other, tenderhearted, forgiving one another, just as God through Christ has forgiven you. Ephesians 4:31-32 NLT
- Therefore a man shall leave his father and mother and be joined to his wife, and they shall become one flesh. Genesis 2:24 NKJV

Declarations
- We decree and declare that contention and division have no place in our family.
- We decree and declare that as we join as one in marriage, our families will join together as one.
- We decree and declare that when we gather, there will be no strife or separation in Jesus' name.

XVII. Bridal Party

Heavenly Father, we thank and praise You for the joy we are experiencing and for the preparation You are gracing us for! We are so grateful. We know that as we enter into our covenant of marriage and into our wedding, we cannot go without the support of those who You have ordained to support us in this season. So we come to You to pray concerning our bridal party.

First and foremost, Lord, we pray for wisdom, discernment, and the leading of the Holy Spirit in choosing who will stand with us throughout our wedding planning and on our wedding day. Thank You that in Your divine wisdom, You already know how many bridesmaids and groomsmen we will have and who they are, and we thank You that You have already prepared their hearts to support us. Lord, we pray that as we approach them to ask that they support us on this journey, they will realize and know that they were handpicked by You because they are well respected and full of wisdom. We thank You Lord for giving us a bridal party that will sharpen and water us and stick close to us as we go through our preparations.

We pray for the spirit of unity in our bridal party. We come against any seeds of drama or discord that the enemy will try to sow, and we declare that brotherly love will reign in our bridal party. Lord, thank You that our bridal party will partake in the joyous celebration we will have on our wedding day. May You bless them with all of the resources they need to support us, and may they feel joy in this process rather than stress. Lord, we pray that they will help us watch and pray in this season as we enter into a new chapter of our lives. We pray especially for our best man, and maid/matron of honor, that You will give them the grace of coordination and planning. We trust that everything they do for us will be a blessing, and that they will reap one hundred fold. May everyone in our bridal party be refreshed by each other's company. We thank You for their lives, and we thank You that they will continue to see Your goodness in the land of the living. In Jesus' name, Amen!

Scriptures

- Walk with the wise and become wise, for a companion of fools suffers harm. Proverbs 13:20 NIV
- As iron sharpens iron, So a man sharpens the countenance of his friend. Proverbs 27:17 NKJV
- One who has unreliable friends soon comes to ruin, but there is a friend who sticks closer than a brother. Proverbs 18:24 NIV
- Let brotherly love continue. Hebrews 13:1 KJV
- The bride, a princess, looks glorious in her golden gown. In her beautiful robes, she is led to the king, accompanied by her bridesmaids. What a joyful and enthusiastic procession as they enter the king's palace! Psalms 45:13-15 NLT
- Your love has given me great joy and encouragement, because you, brother, have refreshed the hearts of the Lord's people. Philemon 1:7 NIV
- Yet I am confident I will see the Lord's goodness while I am here in the land of the living. Psalms 27:13 NLT

Declarations

- We decree and declare that our bridal party is hand-picked by God and that each member is equipped to fulfill a unique role in the bridal party.
- We decree and declare that our bridal party will work together and that they are graced to assist us in this season.

- We decree and declare that each member of our bridal party is blessed and that they will reap every good thing they sow into us in Jesus' name.

XVIII. Officiants and Counselors

Dear Father, we are so grateful for Your grace that has brought us this far, and we thank You for the guidance and counsel You have allowed us to have access to as we prepare to join in marriage. As we avail ourselves to receive Godly counsel, we pray that You give us the grace to be transparent, and we pray that You give us victory over anything that seeks to divide us. We pray against pride, and we pray for the grace to humble ourselves so that we can gladly receive Your instruction and correction. Lord, we know that the counseling process will require us to be open and honest with ourselves and with each other. We know that we might receive rebuke and correction. We know that we might hear things that we do not want to hear. But we ask for Your divine help and grace to submit to this process, because we know that if we do not listen to the teachings that we receive, we will be like the foolish man that built his house on the sand. Holy Spirit, we ask You to come and dwell in our counseling sessions. Brood over every conversation and reveal the deep and hidden things that need to be addressed. We thank You in advance for having Your own perfect way in our midst.

Lord, we also pray for our marriage counselors and officiants and ask that according to Your Word, they will feed us with knowledge and understanding about the covenant we are entering into. We pray that You will strengthen them as they avail themselves to counsel us. Lord, we thank You that through their counsel and advice, You have ordained that our marriage will be victorious. We thank You that because of the wisdom and insight You have given them for us, our marriage will stand firm and be established. We pray, Father, that as they pour into our lives and future, You will exalt Yourself in their lives and blanket their lives with Your glory. May they experience unending success in life and marriage in the name of Jesus. We thank You for the gift of wise counsel, and as they continue to bless many marriages, may their marriages forever be blessed. In Jesus' name, Amen.

Scriptures
- Where there is no [wise, intelligent] guidance, the people fall [and go off course like a ship without a helm], But in the abundance of [wise and godly] counselors there is victory. Proverbs 11:14 AMP
- Without counsel purposes are disappointed: But in the multitude of counsellers they are established. Proverbs 15:22 KJV
- Plans succeed through good counsel; don't go to war without wise advice. Proverbs 20:18 NLT
- "Anyone who listens to my teaching and follows it is wise, like a person who builds a house on solid rock. Though the rain comes in torrents and the floodwaters rise and the winds beat against that house, it won't collapse because it is built on bedrock. But anyone who hears my teaching and doesn't obey it is foolish, like a person who builds a house on sand. When the rains and floods come and the winds beat against that house, it will collapse with a mighty crash." Matthew 7:24-27 NLT
- But as it is written: "Eye has not seen, nor ear heard, Nor have entered into the heart of man the things which God has prepared for those who love Him." But God has revealed them to us through His Spirit. For the Spirit searches all things, yes, the deep things of God. 1 Corinthians 2:9-10 NKJV

- And I will give you pastors according to mine heart, which shall feed you with knowledge and understanding. Jeremiah 3:15 KJV

Declarations
- We decree and declare that we will submit to the process of learning and unlearning as we go through counseling.
- We decree and declare that our counseling will be fruitful and equip us for a lifetime of successful marriage in Jesus' name.
- We decree and declare that as our marriage counselors and officiants are pouring into us, their marriages will be blessed and watered in Jesus' name.

XIX. Guests and Gift Givers

Lord, we are so grateful that we can look forward to our wedding day. It is a beautiful day that You have made and we will rejoice and be glad in it! Father, we commit all of our guests into Your hands. Thank You for giving us a community that is willing to celebrate us as we celebrate! Thank You for giving us family members and friends who are rejoicing as we are rejoicing. We thank You for giving us a reason to be joyful, and we pray that this joy will dwell in the hearts of all of our guests. We pray that as all of our family and friends celebrate us, you give them many reasons to celebrate! We pray that You will bring joy and peace to their lives in abundance in the mighty name of Jesus. We thank You for their lives and for their heart toward us. Bless them and increase them mightily in Jesus' name.

Lord, we also pray for every person who will sow financially into our marriage. Your Word says that a generous man shall be prosperous and enriched – that those who water will also be watered, reaping the generosity they have sown. We pray that everyone who gives us a gift will receive the measure of that gift pressed down, shaken together, and running over! By reason of their generosity, may lack be gone from all of their lives in the name of Jesus! Jesus, You said that it is more blessed to give than to receive. May all of our guests and gift givers receive spiritual and financial blessings in abundance. Thank You in advance for doing it in their lives. In Jesus' name, Amen!

Scriptures
- This is the day the Lord has made. We will rejoice and be glad in it. Psalms 118:24 NLT
- Rejoice with those who rejoice; mourn with those who mourn. Romans 12:15 NIV

- All the days of the afflicted are bad, But a glad heart has a continual feast [regardless of the circumstances]. Proverbs 15:15 AMP
- The generous man [is a source of blessing and] shall be prosperous and enriched, And he who waters will himself be watered [reaping the generosity he has sown]. Proverbs 11:25 AMP
- "Give, and you will receive. Your gift will return to you in full—pressed down, shaken together to make room for more, running over, and poured into your lap. The amount you give will determine the amount you get back." Luke 6:38 NLT
- "Do to others whatever you would like them to do to you." Matthew 7:12a NLT
- And remember the words of the Lord Jesus, that He said, 'It is more blessed to give than to receive.' Acts 20:35b NJKV

Declarations

- We decree and declare that our guests and those who have sown in our lives will be blessed abundantly for their sacrifice of sowing into our lives.
- We decree and declare that those who have celebrated us will always be celebrated in Jesus' name.
- We decree and declare that the lives of our guests are filled with joy and peace in Jesus' name.

XX. Vendors

Lord Jesus, we thank You again for the abundant blessings You have planned for us on our wedding day. We are praying that Your glory will be seen on that day. As we prepare, we cannot do it on our own. We pray that You will help us to select a spirit-filled and skilled team of vendors who will assist in our vision of glorifying You and You alone. Holy Spirit, You are the one who has given various talents to Your people. As we select our wedding planner, photographer, videographer, DJ, dressmaker, suit maker, makeup artists, hair stylists, barber, musicians, emcee, cake baker, florist, stationer, caterer, special effects designers, and all other vendors, we pray that You will guide us to those who You have anointed to serve our vision on our wedding day. We thank You in advance for leading us to whom You see fit. We put this totally into Your hands. Let our fleshy preferences and desires give way to Your perfect will, for we know that our wedding day will be a highly spiritual moment, and we do not want there to be any interference in the name of Jesus. We pray for the spirit of discernment, and We glorify You that all things have already worked out for our good.

Lord, we pray a special prayer of blessing over the vendors You have ordained to serve us in our wedding planning and on our wedding day. We pray that as You anointed the hands of Bezalel, You anoint our vendors with great wisdom, ability, and expertise. We pray that You will anoint their hands and that their craftsmanship will produce wealth in the name of Jesus. Lord, let them not just be gifted, but let them be anointed and appointed to win souls for Your kingdom. As they exercise their various talents, may the spirit of wisdom be their partner in entrepreneurship. May they be Kingdom influencers and build an empire for You. Lord, may they be at the top of their mountain of influence. May they never be drawn away by temptations in their industry. Strengthen their hands for their work. Father, we pray that as You have uniquely gifted them, they will rise and be promoted. May they use their gifts for kings in Jesus' name. Enlarge the coasts of their businesses and enlarge their territory. May they increase in their skills and hear You clearly at all times. Lord, as our vendors serve us on our wedding day, may their businesses be blessed and may the desires of their hearts be fulfilled.

Through our vendors, may Your Spirit find its home in every room that matters concerning our wedding will enter. As our cake is being made and eaten, may Your glory fill the atmosphere. As we take pictures and videos, may Your Spirit fill the venue. As our DJ plays and we dance and celebrate, may Your name be lifted and may sorrow flee. As the hairstylists and makeup artists work, may Your peace reign. Lord take complete control, and we will be careful to give You all of the glory and honor for Your wondrous works. Thank You Lord for Your blessings over our vendors. In Jesus' name, Amen!

Scriptures
- There are different kinds of gifts, but the same Spirit distributes them. 1 Corinthians 12:4 NIV
- Each of you should use whatever gift you have received to serve others, as faithful stewards of God's grace in its various forms. 1 Peter 4:10 NIV
- Then the Lord said to Moses, "Look, I have specifically chosen Bezalel son of Uri, grandson of Hur, of the tribe of Judah. I have filled him with the Spirit of God, giving him great wisdom, ability, and expertise in all kinds of crafts. He is a master craftsman, expert in working with gold, silver, and bronze. He is skilled in engraving and mounting

- gemstones and in carving wood. He is a master at every craft!" Exodus 31:1-5 NLT
- Instruct all the skilled craftsmen whom I have filled with the spirit of wisdom. Have them make garments for Aaron that will distinguish him as a priest set apart for my service. Exodus 28:3 NLT
- But remember the LORD your God, for it is he who gives you the ability to produce wealth, and so confirms his covenant, which he swore to your ancestors, as it is today. Deuteronomy 8:18 NIV
- They were all trying to frighten us, thinking, "Their hands will get too weak for the work, and it will not be completed." But I prayed, "Now strengthen my hands." Nehemiah 6:9 NIV
- If you are uniquely gifted in your work, you will rise and be promoted. You won't be held back—you'll stand before kings! Proverbs 22:29 TPT

<u>Declarations</u>
- We decree and declare that our vendors are gifted by God and anointed to make our wedding day a blessing.
- We decree and declare that as our vendors avail themselves to make our wedding day a success, the works of their hands are forever blessed.
- We decree and declare that our vendors' businesses will continue to grow and thrive in Jesus' name.

XXI. Beautiful Day/ Weather

Dear Lord, we thank You for Your sovereignty and Your mercy. Thank You for seeing it fit to bring us to this point in our journey. As we look toward our wedding day, we know that it is a day that You have made, and we will rejoice in Your grace and faithfulness. We commit the day to You, and we pray that Your glory will rise and overshadow everything we do. Let Your light drive away all darkness and gloom. We pray that the day will be beautiful, joyous, and full of laughter and that all of our guests will feel Your presence.

We commit the weather into Your hands. We pray against any inclement weather that will frustrate us, and we rebuke every plan of the enemy to bring us shame or hindrances through the weather. We pray that the weather will be exactly as You will it to be on our day and that the Holy Spirit will go before us and make all things beautiful. Whether we experience showers of blessing or beaming sunshine, help us to be at peace, knowing that You have ordained every detail. We thank You in advance that our wedding day will be a beautiful day to remember. In Jesus' name, Amen!

Scriptures
- Arise, shine; For your light has come! And the glory of the Lord is risen upon you. Isaiah 60:1 NKJV
- This is the Lord's doing, and it is wonderful to see. This is the day the Lord has made. We will rejoice and be glad in it. Psalms 118:23-24 NLT
- The Lord does whatever pleases him, in the heavens and on the earth, in the seas and all their depths. He makes clouds rise from the ends of the earth; he sends lightning with the

- rain and brings out the wind from his storehouses. Psalms 135:6-7 NIV
- He decided how hard the winds should blow and how much rain should fall. He made the laws for the rain and laid out a path for the lightning. Then he saw wisdom and evaluated it. He set it in place and examined it thoroughly. Job 28:25-27 NLT
- But He said to them, "Why are you fearful, O you of little faith?" Then He arose and rebuked the winds and the sea, and there was a great calm. So the men marveled, saying, "Who can this be, that even the winds and the sea obey Him?" Matthew 8:26-27 NKJV
- His Spirit made the heavens beautiful, and his power pierced the gliding serpent. These are just the beginning of all that he does, merely a whisper of his power. Who, then, can comprehend the thunder of his power? Job 26:13-14 NLT

Declarations
- We decree and declare that our wedding day is a beautiful day of much sunshine and joy.
- We decree and declare that our wedding will not be hindered by inclement weather, but that the weather will be subject to the will of God in Jesus' name.

XXII. Physical and Spiritual Territories

Dear Lord, there is no one like You in Heaven or on the earth. You are so faithful, and we thank You for bringing us together as a couple to fulfill Your will on this earth. Thank You for delighting in every step we take and for taking control over every aspect of our marriage. We come now to ask for Your guidance in identifying the physical and spiritual territories we should take for Your Kingdom as we embark on our union as husband and wife. Holy Spirit, we ask that You direct us in the way that we should go.

Lord, we pray first for Your guidance regarding the physical location where we should live as a newlywed couple. In Your Word, You speak of Your people dwelling in peaceful and secure homes, where they will enjoy fruitfulness, rest, and blessings. We avail ourselves to hear Your voice concerning where we should live, and we pray that as we obey Your voice to go there, our going there will accomplish all that You intend it to accomplish. We pray that Your hand will be evident in the process and that no hindrances will take place. We soak our marital home in the blood of Jesus. We pray that it will always be territory that is conducive to the presence of the Holy Spirit. We come against any contrary, territorial spirit dwelling near our home, and we decree and declare that wherever we live will be Kingdom territory.

<u>Scriptures</u>
- The steps of a good man are ordered by the LORD, And He delights in his way. Psalms 37:23 NKJV
- My people will live in peaceful dwelling places, in secure homes, in undisturbed places of rest. Isaiah 32:18 NIV

- In those days people will live in the houses they build and eat the fruit of their own vineyards. Unlike the past, invaders will not take their houses and confiscate their vineyards. For my people will live as long as trees, and my chosen ones will have time to enjoy their hard-won gains. Isaiah 65:21-22 NLT
- And I will provide a place for my people Israel and will plant them so that they can have a home of their own and no longer be disturbed. Wicked people will not oppress them anymore, as they did at the beginning. 2 Samuel 7:10 NIV
- Blessed shall you be in the city, and blessed shall you be in the country. Deuteronomy 28:3 NKJV
- "And if it seems evil to you to serve the LORD, choose for yourselves this day whom you will serve, whether the gods which your fathers served that were on the other side of the River, or the gods of the Amorites, in whose land you dwell. But as for me and my house, we will serve the LORD." Joshua 24:15 NKJV
- Now the blood shall be a sign for you on the houses where you are. And when I see the blood, I will pass over you; and the plague shall not be on you to destroy you when I strike the land of Egypt. Exodus 12:13 NKJV
- Every place on which the sole of your foot treads shall be yours: from the wilderness and Lebanon, from the river, the River Euphrates, even to the Western Sea, shall be your territory. Deuteronomy 11:24 NKJV
- Behold, I give unto you power to tread on serpents and scorpions, and over all the power of the enemy: and nothing shall by any means hurt you. Luke 10:19 KJV
- Arise, walk through the land in the length of it and in the breadth of it; for I will give it unto thee. Genesis 13:17 KJV

Declarations
- We decree and declare that our family will forever and ever serve and submit to the Lord Jesus Christ.
- We decree and declare that wherever the soles of our feet tread will be kingdom territory in Jesus' name.
- We decree and declare that we will take over spiritual territory for Christ in Jesus' name.

XXIII. A Beautiful and Glorious Marriage and Legacy

Dear Father, we are grateful for the opportunity to begin a new legacy in our generation through our marriage. We thank You that before we were even conceived, You knew that our destinies would be knitted together. We praise Your name because we know that without Your grace and mercy, we would not be here.

We thank You for Your mercies that are new in our lives every morning. Lord, we ask that You have mercy on us if we have ever perceived our marriage to be anything other than ordained by You, for Your will, purpose, and glory. We are most grateful that You have seen it fit for us to destroy the kingdom of darkness together and manifest Your Kingdom on this earth. We yield to this Kingdom assignment, and we pray for the grace to fear You and You alone. We pray that we will not succumb to culture's view of marriage, but that we will pattern our marriage after the Holy Bible—our source of instruction and guidance—after Your rhema Word to us, and after the leadings of the Holy Spirit. We pray that as we establish a new order of obedience and submission through our marriage, You will extend mercies to our children, our children's children, and all of the generations that follow us. We ask, O Lord, that You will bless our union and ALL that our union produces in Jesus' name.

Father, we ask for Your grace to rule over nations and kingdoms. We pray that we will be daily empowered to root out, pull down, destroy, and throw down all demonic altars or evil patterns that have been established in our bloodlines. We pray that we will be daily empowered to build and to plant altars of prayer, praise, and sacrifice. We pray that, through our submission to Christ, Godly patterns will be created in our bloodline. We pray that we will be able to leave not only a legacy of wealth and riches for generations to come, but also a legacy of prayer, deadly commitment to Christ, and good works for the Kingdom of God. We pray that we will walk in integrity all the days of our marriage and lives, and that our children will be blessed. We pray for grace to train our children in Your ways so that when they are old, they will not depart from You.

Lord, we commit our legacy to You. May the grace for consistency and the fire of the Holy Spirit be released on us as we enter this marriage covenant. May we die to our flesh and our own desires so that our marriage may bear much fruit. We pray that we will be planted in Your House and flourish in Your courts all of our days. In old age, may we be able to sit together and say that we have pleased God, and may we be fresh and flourishing. May we make an impact for Christ in our lifetime, and may our union be remembered for good. May we always testify that as we live for You, we see Your goodness in the land of the living. May we live in the promise of Exodus 23:25-26, that as we serve You, You will bless our bread and water, take sicknesses and illnesses away from us, remove miscarriages and barrenness from us, and fulfill the number of our days. May we experience 100 years of marriage and an eternity of peace.

We thank You for Your precious promises. Thank You God for establishing Your Kingdom through us. We commit and dedicate our marriage to You, and we know that You will keep it. In Jesus' name, Amen!

Scriptures

- "I knew you before I formed you in your mother's womb." Jeremiah 1:5a NLT
- Yet I still dare to hope when I remember this: The faithful love of the Lord never ends! His mercies never cease. Great is his faithfulness; his mercies begin afresh each morning. Lamentations 3:21-23 NLT
- The Son of God appeared for this purpose, to destroy the works of the devil. 1 John 3:8b AMP
- But the mercy of the Lord is from everlasting to everlasting on those who fear Him, And His righteousness to children's children, To such as keep His covenant, And to those who remember His commandments to do them. Psalms 103:17-18 NKJV
- Praise the Lord! Blessed is the man who fears the Lord, Who delights greatly in His commandments. His descendants will be mighty on earth; The generation of the upright will be blessed. Psalms 112:1-2 NKJV
- See, I have this day set you over the nations and over the kingdoms, To root out and to pull down, To destroy and to throw down, To build and to plant. Jeremiah 1:10 NKJV
- A good man leaves an inheritance to his children's children. Proverbs 13:22a NKJV
- The godly walk with integrity; blessed are their children who follow them. Proverbs 20:7 NLT
- Train up a child in the way he should go, And when he is old he will not depart from it. Proverbs 22:6 NKJV
- Verily, verily, I say unto you, Except a corn of wheat fall into the ground and die, it abideth alone: but if it die, it bringeth forth much fruit. John 12:24 KJV

- Those who are planted in the house of the Lord shall flourish in the courts of our God. They shall still bear fruit in old age; They shall be fresh and flourishing. Psalms 92:13-14 NKJV
- The one thing I ask of the Lord—the thing I seek most—is to live in the house of the Lord all the days of my life, delighting in the Lord's perfections and meditating in his Temple. Psalms 27:4 NLT
- And the Lord said, "My Spirit shall not strive with man forever, for he is indeed flesh; yet his days shall be one hundred and twenty years." Genesis 6:3 NKJV
- "For the mountains shall depart and the hills be removed, but My kindness shall not depart from you, nor shall My covenant of peace be removed," says the Lord, who has mercy on you. Isaiah 54:10 NJKV
- For I know whom I have believed, and am persuaded that he is able to keep that which I have committed unto him against that day. 2 Timothy 1:12b KJV

Declarations
- We decree and declare that our marriage will be a blessing to this generation.
- We decree and declare that our descendants will be blessed and mighty on the earth.
- We decree and declare that we will train up our children to serve the Lord, and in so doing, we will establish a new order of submission and service in our bloodline.
- We decree and declare that through our submission to the Holy Spirit, we will be able to leave an inheritance of Godliness for our children's children, and generations to come in Jesus' name.
- We decree and declare that we will enjoy 100+ years of marital bliss and Kingdom influence in Jesus' name!

About the Author

Tatiana Natasha Codner is a Christian, a lover of all things Kingdom, and a wife. Tatiana has experienced the transformative power of prayer and declarations in her life and is passionate about sharing the love of Christ with others. By the grace of God, Tatiana holds a Bachelor's degree in Criminology from the University of Pennsylvania and a law degree from Fordham University School of Law. Tatiana is an attorney in New York where she currently resides with her husband and best friend Delano Codner.

www.ingramcontent.com/pod-product-compliance
Lightning Source LLC
Chambersburg PA
CBHW070735230426
43665CB00016B/2251